GRANITE CITY
GRANITE CITY
GRANITE CITY
GRANITE CITY
01224 - 587065

Granite City Fish

Maureen Forbes-Gray

Photography Berry Bingel and Stuart Johnstone

Printers Harley & Cox Ltd. Dundee

I was born and bred in the North East of Scotland where fishing has been a way of life for generations. Fresh fish, from North East Fish Markets, is still delivered to my doorstep every Friday morning. This tradition stretches back into my childhood when I remember my mother buying fish at the door of the family home.

The Fishing industry has been a backbone of our society, and a way of life, for generations of people throughout this area.

Ed Fletcher took over the family business, Granite City Fish from his parents, and his success has generously financed the production of this book. This allows all proceeds from this book to be donated to the Grampian Autistic Society. An organisation which funds the essential work of dedicated carers, research programmes and support structures for the struggling families, coping with children who have Autism.

Autism is a very complex syndrome in which the main problem is communicating with others in a meaningful way. This can lead to a variety of sometimes disturbing or bizarre behaviours, which are often distressing for the children, and those who come in contact with them.

It gives me great pleasure to have the opportunity to create the Granite City Fish cook book. It not only supports this year's fisheries showcase event, but also raises money and awareness for Autism.

To Alexander
who taught me to
abandon all assumptions

To James
whose drawings helped me understand
the 'Art of Conversation'

And To Michael
who showed me that feelings
are as infinite as colour

By Carol Gray
Consultant to Students
with Autism Spectrum Disorders
Jenison, America.

Contents

CONTENTS continued

The Aberdeen Harbour

Set like a gem
Twixt the Don and Dee
The Silver City by the
North Sea.

This book is dedicated to our
parents Ted and Gina Fletcher.
Our achievements in life reflect the love and support
they have given us over the last 40 years.
May they have a long, happy and prosperous life.

Love from John and June
Ed and Susan
and all your grandchildren.

Granite City Fish

Foreword - Dr Margaret Farquhar JP-Lord Provost of Aberdeen

What could be more appropriate than a collection of fish recipes from the North East of Scotland?

You will find within these pages many exciting ideas for preparing and eating fish and seafood dishes. In addition to being a guide to enjoying fish, the book is also part of a celebration of an industry which is one of the most challenging and demanding occupations there is. In our part of Scotland fish has always been an important source of nourishment, employment and prosperity. Around our coastline fishing continues to form the backbone of many communities which brave the hostile environment of the North Sea to harvest the finest fish and seafood available. It is they who provide the raw materials which have been transformed by our team of chefs into tempting dishes you will find inside. It is to all those who work in the industry, onshore and offshore, that I would like to dedicate Aberdeen City Council's contribution.

My personal thanks go to everyone, particularly Ed Fletcher who has played a part in making this book a reality. It has been a real team effort involving the industry, the Council and a number of individuals who simply love fish. And of course special thanks must go to our teams of chefs who have given their time and their skills to make this project a reality.

I would also like to thank everyone who buys the book as all the proceeds will go to a most worthy cause - The Grampian Autistic Society.

I hope that you will enjoy this book and will be tempted to recreate some of the recipes. You will be glad you did.

Rick Stein

Chickpea Parsley and Salt Cod Stew

I met Rick Stein at his Ottakar's book launch in Aberdeen this year, and thoroughly enjoyed his fish cookery demonstration, I am delighted that he has given us one of his recipes. This dish is a fitting start to this fish cookery book which celebrates the fisheries showcase event taking part in Aberdeen this year.

Serves 4

Ingredients

750 g / 1 1/2 lb unskinned cod fillet

350 g / 12 oz dried chick peas

175 g / 6 oz potato, peeled

85 ml / 3 fl oz olive oil

8 garlic cloves, finely chopped

1 teaspoon dried chilli flakes

4 plum tomatoes, roughly chopped

3 - 4 tablespoons chopped flat leafed parsley

Salt and freshly ground black pepper

Salt the cod overnight (ask advice from your fishmonger or see page 238 in Rick Stein's book 'Seafood Odyssey')

Cover the chick peas in plenty of water and leave them to soak overnight, too.

The next day drain the chick peas and pour over enough fresh water to cover them by about 5cm (2 inches) Bring to the boil, add the peeled potato and simmer until tender, adding hot water now and then if necessary to make sure they stay covered. Drain and set aside, saving the liquid.

Drop the salt cod into a pan of boiling water and simmer for 6 -8 minutes or until just cooked. Drain, and when cool enough to handle, flake the flesh into large pieces discarding the skin and any bones.

Heat the olive oil in a large pan, add the garlic and chilli flakes and cook for a minute or two without browning. Add the tomatoes, chick peas and potato, which should be broken up into small pieces with the back of a wooden spoon.

Add a little of the cooking liquid from the chick peas and 300 ml (10 fl oz) of water and simmer for 20 - 30 minutes until the stew has reduced and thickened a little.

Gently fold in the salt cod and parsley and season liberally with fresh ground black pepper.

Taste the stew for salt, but you probably won't need any.

Having been brought up in the North East of Scotland, salt cod is something I am most familiar with and always enjoy it. My friend's in Shetland still hang salt fish on the washing line to dry out! It really is a wonderful sight!

Footnote: Apologies to the reader on what might appear to be a confusing soup of metric and imperial measurements that appear in this book. I have faithfully adhered to the recipes provided to me by the chefs.

Ardoe House Hotel
Hot Smoked Monkfish in a Seafood Bouillabaisse with Saffron Potato

Serves 4

Ingredients

4 x 140 g / 5 oz boneless trimmed monkfish portions

4 x sea scallops

4 x king prawns

12 x mussels

Bouillabaisse

1 leek (julienne)

2 carrots (julienne)

3 shallots (finely chopped)

2 tomatoes (de- seeded and diced)

2 cloves garlic

2 sprigs thyme

1 oz / 30g finely chopped parsley

150 ml white wine

250 ml fish stock

50g / 1 1/2 oz unsalted butter

1 pinch saffron threads

juice of lemon

seasoning

Saffron Potato

4 medium potatoes

3g of saffron

For the Monkfish:

Place the monkfish portions in a hot smoking tin using oak chips leave until nicely browned, it may need to be cooked a little more in the oven. (Alternatively you can use roast monkfish instead of smoked)

To make the Bouillabaisse:

Sweat shallots, garlic, carrot leeks and tomatoes in a little butter, do not brown. Add the white wine, fish stock, saffron, lemon, thyme and parsley reduce by 1/3 and gradually add the remainder of the butter. Season.

For the Shellfish:

Sauté the king prawns and scallops in butter, add the mussels and a little bouillabaisse liquor till the mussels open.

To prepare the Saffron Potatoes:

Peel and cut the potatoes into a round shape using a round pastry cutter. Bring to boil in salted water with saffron threads, simmer until cooked through. (see picture on how to serve potato)

To serve:

Divide the seafood equally between four heated bowls, ladle some of the bouillabaisse over the top, serve immediately.

The Cock and Bull Restaurant
Poached Fruits of the Sea, Ravioli of Crab and Basil Infused in a Light Saffron Nage

Serves 4

Seafood required
8 scallops
8 langoustine tails
12 mussels
8 oz salmon fillet
8 oz monkfish

Nage
2 pints fresh fish stock
125 ml Noilly Pratt
1 generous pinch of saffron
2 oz cubed butter (cold)
4 small shallots (finely chopped)

Ravioli of crab
8½ oz plain flour
2 whole eggs
3 egg yolks
1 tablespoon olive oil
salt to taste

Filling for Ravioli
6 oz crab meat
2 oz salmon fillet
1 egg white
6 basil leaves shredded
salt, cayenne pepper
lemon juice to taste

Garnish
8 asparagus spears
2 medium carrots
1 leek

Cut the salmon and monkfish into 4 equal pieces, place the shallots in the bottom of a flat pan, and place the seafood over them. Place the seafood carefully so that they can be removed easily, when cooked. Pour the cold fish stock and Noilly Pratt over the fish and season with salt and pepper. Place the fish in the fridge to chill, for cooking later.

Place the seafood on a medium heat to poach the fish, drain of the cooking liquor when cooked and add the saffron to it. Reduce this by half in another pan, pass through a fine sieve and finish by adding the cold butter one lump at a time to the nage, to give it a rich taste and consistency.

To make the pasta dough:
Take the flour, eggs olive oil and salt and place in a mixing bowl. Lightly mix on low speed, until well mixed, then place the dough on a lightly floured surface, and knead till you have a smooth paste. Rest dough in the fridge for one hour.

Using the minimum setting on the pasta machine roll out the pasta, and cut into 8 discs. Place all filling ingredients in a food processor and process till smooth, check seasoning. Place a good portion in the centre of four of the discs, cover with the other disc and seal the edge with your finger and thumb, crimping the edges shut. Place in a pan of boiling water and cook for three minutes. Remove from the pan refresh in cold water and cool.

Garnish:
Cut carrot and leek into julienne-use a mandolin if possible. Then blanch in boiling water for a few seconds, and refresh in cold water to retain the colour. Blanch the asparagus in the same way, but leaving them whole.

To serve:
Add the asparagus and vegetables to the nage, heat through. Place the ravioli in a little salted water and heat through. Warm four deep bowls, divide the fish equally between them, place the julienne of vegetables on top of the fish Add the ravioli and place the asparagus over this and pour over the saffron nage.

1995
ÔTES DU LUBERON
Appellation Côtes du Luberon
CE OF FRANCE
ellier de Marrenon
MIS EN BOUTEILLE PAR LES PRODUCTEURS
La Tour d'Aigues (Vaucluse) France

Copthorne Hotel Aberdeen
Seared Salmon
with Saffron Rissoto and a Parmesan Crisp

Serves 4

Risotto

250 g / 8 oz of risotto rice

50 ml olive oil

800 ml fish stock

125 ml white wine

1g saffron

2 shallots, finely diced

Salmon

4 x 150 g fillets of salmon (pinboned)

25 ml olive oil

Parmesan Crisps

50 g / 2 oz finely grated parmesan

50 g / 2 oz dried parmesan

1 x tablespoon poppy seeds

Pesto - blend the following:

50 g / 2 oz toasted pine kernels

75 g / 2 1/2 oz fresh basil

200 ml olive oil

25 g / 1 oz peeled garlic

To prepare risotto:
Sweat shallots in the oil until transparent then add rice and sweat for a further minute. Add the saffron. Add the wine and stock gradually letting the liquor absorb totally to ensure a creamy consistency. Simmer for 12 minutes.

To prepare the salmon:
Heat a heavy based frying pan and add some oil. When it starts to smoke add the salmon and cook for 5 minutes then turn over and cook for a further 5 minutes. Remove from the pan and keep warm.

To prepare the Parmesan crisp:
Mix all the ingredients together divide mix into 4 and spread onto a well oiled tray and bake in a hot oven (approx 190C) for 4 minutes. Remove to a cooling rack with a fish slice. Allow to cool.

To serve:
On four warmed plates, place the risotto in the centre of the plate, top with the salmon, drizzle the pesto sauce round the edge of the plate. Top with parmesan crisp.

The Courtyard Restaurant

Darne of Halibut with a Salmon and Dill Soufflé set on Seared Mediterranean Vegetables laced with a Red Pepper Coulis

Serves 4

For the Soufflé

200 g / 7 oz fresh boneless salmon fillet

1 egg white (whisked)

30 ml brandy

20 g / oz salt

10 g / 1/4 oz ground white pepper

1/4 litre double cream

20 g/1 oz fresh dill (finely chopped)

For the halibut

600 g / 20 oz fresh halibut fillets cut in 4 equal portions

1/4 litre white wine

1/4 litre water

juice of two lemons

Mediterranean Vegetables

2 courgettes

2 red peppers

1 aubergine

6 shallots

Salt and ground white pepper to taste

2 cloves garlic

olive oil

20 g / 1 oz fresh chopped basil

Red Pepper Coulis

6 whole red peppers

100 g / 3 1/2 oz chopped onions

2 cloves of garlic

olive oil

1 litre vegetable stock

50 ml white wine

Salt and ground white pepper to taste

Lea and Perrins to taste

For the Soufflé:

Cut the salmon fillet into small pieces and place in a food processor. Add the whisked egg, brandy, salt and pepper, process to a smooth consistency in the processor, add the cream slowly, processing again to a smooth consistency. Add the dill and cool in the refrigerator for 20 minutes.

For the halibut:

Cut the halibut into 4 equal portions and place in a shallow casserole dish. Place the cooled salmon mixture into a piping bag with a star nozzle and pipe the soufflé on top of the halibut. Spread the soufflé evenly, place in the fridge until ready to cook.

Place the above ingredients in a shallow dish, bake in the oven with the soufflé piped on top at 180°C for approximately 15-20 minutes or until the soufflé takes colour.

Mediterranean Vegetables:

Cut the courgettes, red peppers, aubergine and shallots into equal pieces (approx 2cm by 2cm). Mince the garlic and sauté everything together, with the olive oil and seasoning in the pan. Chop the fresh basil stir through one minute before serving.

Red Pepper Coulis:

Chop the red peppers, onion and garlic, add to hot olive oil and seal the vegetables, add the vegetable stock, white wine, Lea & Perrins to taste and seasoning, simmer until the peppers are soft.

Food process the sauce to a smooth puree, strain back into the pot, season.

To serve:

Place the vegetables in the middle of a warmed plate, top with the halibut surround with the red pepper coulis. Serve with boiled new potatoes.

VALE

The Green Inn Ballater

Winner of The Trophée D' Argent for the following Recipes representing Grampian Region
An assiette of fish from the Peterhead and Aberdeen Fish Market

Ham and Haddie - Tatties and Herrin - Tweed Kettle

Serves 4

Ham and Taddie

4 x 2 oz finnan haddock fillet
4 fl oz milk
1 oz unsalted butter
2 oz chopped chives
2 fl oz olive oil
ground black pepper
4 x 1 oz pieces of Ayrshire bacon

Tatties and Herrin

4 small herrin fillets
4 juniper berries
4 small bay leaves
4 white peppercorns
1/4 pint white wine
4 x 1oz tattie scones
2 oz onion confit
Caviar

Confit Onions

3 lb sliced red onions
10 oz demerara sugar
7 fl oz cassis (double strength ribena can be used instead)
2 fl oz sherry vinegar
1 oz salt
2 fl oz oil

Tweed Kettle

4 oz washed kale
30 g butter
6 fl oz fish stock
4 fl oz dry white wine
6 oz cream
2 oz chopped spring onion
1 oz chopped dill
4 medium langoustine tails
4 x 2 oz medallions middle cut salmon
salt and pepper

Ham and Taddie:
Poach the haddock in the milk and butter, mix the chopped chives and oil with the black pepper. Pan fry the bacon. Finally, dress the haddock and bacon on the plate., and mask with the chive oil.

Herrin:
Wash herrin. Make court bouillon with bay leaves, juniper berries, pepper corns, white wine and 1/4 pint water, gently simmer herrin in court bouillon for 4 minutes. Pan fry the potato scones, heat the onion confit.

Place the potato scones on a warm plate, place onion confit on the scone. Place two pieces of herrin on top of the onion confit. Top with a teaspoon of caviar.

To prepare Onion Confit:
Fry the onions in the oil and demerara sugar, cassis and sherry vinegar. Add the salt and cook to marmalade consistency.

Tweed Kettle:
Blanch the kale then sauté in butter and season. Reduce the fish stock and wine by half, add cream and reduce by a further half. Add spring onion and dill, season with salt and pepper.

Pan fry the langoustine tail and salmon, the salmon should be slightly underdone. Dress the salmon on the buttered kale, top with langoustine place sauce on the side.

The Lairhillock
Warm Crab and Chilli Pasta with Sauteed Langoustine Tails

Serves 4

For the pasta

Either use a good quality fresh spaghetti or make as follows:

300 g / 10oz pasta flour

3 whole eggs

1 egg yolk

Ingredients

16 medium to large langoustines

2 medium onions

1 dried bayleaf or 2/3 fresh

1/2 red or green chilli

1 red pepper

1 clove garlic

3 oz butter

2 dressed crabs (use fresh from the market that day)

juice of 2 limes

small handful of torn basil leaves

seasoning

plain flour

2 oz clarified butter

8 rocket leaves

For the pasta dough:

Beat the eggs. Put the flour in a bowl and add the eggs to make a firm dough and work it well. Remove from bowl and wrap the dough I cling film and refrigerate for at least 2 hours. The pasta dough will keep in the fridge for 36 hours. After refrigeration run through a pasta machine to form spaghetti and leave over a rack to dry.

For the langoustines:

Shell the langoustines. Place the meat to one side.Crush the shells in a pint of water along with one of the onions roughly chopped and the bayleaf. Bring to the boil and let it reduce by half. Strain and keep to one side.

Finely chop the other onion, chilli, red pepper and garlic. Heat the ordinary butter in a small frying pan and sauté the vegetables over a medium heat till soft without browning. Add the crabmeat, season to taste.

To cook the pasta:

Bring a large pan of well salted water to the boil add the pasta and continue a rapid boil till the pasta is cooked. Drain well and toss with the crab mix and add the lime juice and basil. Check the seasoning and keep warm.

Toss the langoustine tails in plain flour. In a large frying pan melt the clarified butter and sauté over a medium heat till golden.

To serve:

Put two rocket leaves on each plate heap the pasta on top and place 4 langoustines on the pasta.

The Olive Tree Brasserie Restaurant

Grilled Squid
with Sweet Chilli Tomato Cream

Serves 4

For the Sauce

1 teaspoon tomato puree
1 clove garlic (chopped)
4 finger lengths fresh Thyme
1/2 teaspoon ground coriander
1 small chilli (sliced)
3 fl oz white wine
10 fl oz double cream
salt, pepper and honey

Ingredients

16 oz cleaned squid
olive oil

To Serve

4 portions basmati rice pilaff

chopped chives to decorate

To make the sauce:

Lightly grease a small pan, and sauté the tomato puree until it begins to change colour.

Add the garlic, thyme and coriander and cook for a further two minutes.

Add the wine and chopped chilli and reduce by half.

Then add the cream and reduce by one third.

Season with salt, pepper and honey. Return to the stove and re-boil.

Check the flavour and remove the thyme

For the squid:

To prepare the squid ask the fishmonger to clean the squid and cut it into large triangles. Wash the squid in cold water, dry thoroughly and rub lightly all over with olive oil. Place squid under a very hot griddle for 1 1/2 minutes each side. Place the rice in the middle of a warmed plate and pour the sauce around the plate. Take the squid off the griddle and place onto the rice and scatter the chopped chives.

Shish Mahal Restaurant
Mahi Mazedar

Served all over the coast of India

Serves 4

Ingredients
4 fillets of haddock
1 large onion
2 cloves of garlic
225 g / 8 oz tomatoes
1 aubergine
1 courgette
1 red pepper
3 tablespoons olive oil
1/4 teaspoon saffron powder
150 ml / 1/4 pint fish stock
2 dried chilli
40 g / 1/2 oz currants
225 g / 8 oz long grain rice
salt and black pepper
teaspoon ground cumin

To garnish
Chopped fresh parsley
2 slices of lime

Cut the fillet of haddock into 2.5cm / 1inch cubes. Peel and chop the onion and garlic. Slit the tomato skins, cover with boiling water, leave for a few minutes, then peel off skin remove the seeds and dice. Cut the aubergine and courgette into small pieces. De-seed and chop the pepper.

Heat the oil in a pan, add the haddock, onion, garlic, aubergine, courgette and pepper and fry over a high heat for about 4 minutes, stirring gently all the time. Stir the saffron into the stock with 450ml / 3/4 pint of water, then pour into the pan. Bring to the boil.

Crumble the dried chilli, add to the pan and stir in the currants, rice and tomatoes. Season with salt, pepper and cumin, reduce to a low heat. Cover the pan and simmer for about 20-25 minutes, stirring now and again, and adding more water if necessary.

To Serve:
Finely chop the parsley - you will need about 2 tablespoons. Spoon the Mahi Mazedar into a serving dish and sprinkle with the parsley, garnish with the lime slices.

Silver Darling Restaurant
Sake Kasu Marinated Sea Bass with Coconut Green Curry Sauce

Serves 4

Ingredients
4 x 7 oz fillets of sea bass

3 tablespoons vegetable oil

Marinade
A 2 inch piece of fresh ginger

3 cups / 27 fl oz mirun*

2 cups / 18 fl oz sake kasu*
(Japanese white wine)

2 cups / 18 fl oz of tamari* or soy sauce

1 cup / 9 fl oz white miso*

1 cup / 9 fl oz rice vinegar
(not seasoned)

8 tablespoons packed brown sugar

Accompaniment:
Coconut green curry sauce
2 shallots (finely chopped)

1 oz / 30 g green curry powder or paste

1 cup / 9 fl oz chicken stock

1 cup / 9 fl oz coconut puree (can be found in Mark's and Spencer)

20 g / 1 oz butter

To make the marinade:
Peel and chop the ginger. In a blender combine the ginger with the remaining ingredients and blend until smooth

Arrange the sea bass in a dish and pour the marinade over it, turning the fish to coat well. Cover and chill the fish, marinade from 3 hours up to 2 days.

Pre-heat the oven to 200°C 400°F and wrap the handle of a 16 inch non stick skillet with a triple layer of foil, shiny side out if the handle is not ovenproof.

Remove the fish from the marinade, letting the excess marinade fall off, discard the excess marinade. In the non stick skillet heat the oil in the oven until moderately hot but not smoking, and sear the fish on one side only until golden brown, about 3 minutes. With tongs turn the fish over and transfer the skillet to the middle of the oven. Roast the fish until cooked through, 4-6 minutes and serve at once with the curry sauce.

Coconut Green Curry Sauce:
Sweat the shallots in the 20g of butter, until the shallots become transparent in colour. Add chicken stock and reduce by half. Add the coconut puree stirring well. Simmer for 10 minutes, pass through a fine sieve. Serve with the fish.

** available at Japanese shops and mail order specialists.*

Thainstone House Hotel
Pan Roasted Fillet of Red Mullet with Fondant Potatoes Fine Ratatouille Sundried Aubergines with Liquorice Dressing

Serves 4

Ingredients

4 baking potato
3/4 pint chicken stock
2 oz butter
4 oz fine diced aubergine
4 oz fine diced peppers
4 oz fine diced courgettes
6 leafs of basil
pint of tomato juice
1/2 oz butter (to sweat diced vegetables)
2 oz of fresh liquorice
4 tablespoons of olive oil
1 tablespoon of balsamic vinegar
4 x 6 oz fillets of red mullet
salt & pepper
24 thin slices of aubergine

Method:

Peel and cut the potato into a 5cm by 4cm square, place in a thick bottomed pan lined with 2oz of the butter, and cover with the chicken stock, cook over a moderate heat until the liquid has reduced.

Sweat off all the diced vegetables using 1/2 oz of butter, add the fresh basil and tomato juice, reduce until all the liquid has gone, place the ratatouille in a small timbale.

Melt the liquorice in a small pan, add the olive oil and balsamic vinegar and whisk until blended.

Pan fry the mullet skin down in a little olive oil, and bake in the oven for 2 minutes, season.

Place the thinly sliced aubergines onto a baking tray, with a little oil and salt and bake in a low oven for six hours or until golden brown and crispy.

To Serve:

Place the fondant potato to the left of the plate, put the ratatouille next to it, put the mullet central to the potato and ratatouille, place the sun dried aubergines on top of the mullet, finish with the dressing.

THE TOLBOOTH RESTAURANT
Seared Tuna Loin with an Avocado Salsa and Red Pepper Vinaigrette

Serves 4

Ingredients

2lbs Tuna loin
(Blue fin, Yellow fin or Bigeye)
vegetable oil

For the Avocado Salsa

1 large ripe avocado
2 tablespoons lemon juice
4 tablespoons virgin olive oil
1 small bunch coriander
1 small red chilli
2 ripe handsome tomatoes
2 limes
some milled black pepper
some fine sea salt

For the red pepper vinaigrette

2 red peppers
6 tablespoons virgin olive oil
1 tablespoon dijon mustard
1 tablespoon white vinegar
Pinch of paprika
Milled black pepper
Fine seasalt

Cut the tuna loin in 4 even slices, refrigerate until needed

To prepare Avocado Salsa:
Peel and cut the avocado in half, remove the stone and slice the avocado, place in a glass bowl. Pour the lemon juice over (this to prevent discolouration). Add the olive oil and washed coriander leaves. De-seed the chilli and chop finely, add to the bowl. Slice the tomatoes in half, de-seed them, dice evenly and add. Segment the limes and add to the bowl. Season the mixture with some milled black pepper and a little sea salt.

For the Red Pepper Vinaigrette:
Brush the red peppers with a little oil, place on a baking tray in a hot oven until well blistered all over. Remove them and place in a plastic container with a lid on (the heat will steam off the skin). After about 20 minutes and take them out, peel off the skin and take out the seeds. Put the peppers together with the mustard, vinegar and olive oil in a blender, strain through a sieve, add the paprika, season with black pepper and seasalt.

And finally:
If you have a griddle great! If not use a heavy bottomed frying pan. Heat up the pan, it has to be very hot!

Brush the tuna loins with a little vegetable oil and sear in the pan, for about 2 minutes on each side then take then out, and keep warm.

Take four warm plates, spoon the salsa on to the middle of the plate. Put the tuna loin on top of the salsa, and dribble the red pepper vinaigrette around, garnish with some coriander leaves and start eating.....

UDNY ARMS HOTEL NEWBURGH
Pan Seared Scallops with Wilted Spinach and a Chive Butter

Serves 4

Ingredients

2 large shallots
1 fl oz white wine vinegar
4 fl oz white wine
4 fl oz fish stock
6 fl oz double cream
1 small bunch snipped chives
4 oz / 125 g unsalted butter
salt
freshly ground pepper
2 tablespoons olive oil
20 medium scallops (fully trimmed and cleaned)
8 oz / 250 g spinach (lightly blanched and well drained)
pinch nutmeg

To make the sauce:

Sweat the shallots in 1oz of the butter until soft, add the white wine vinegar and the white wine, reduce by approximately 2/3. Add the fish stock reduce again by approximately 2/3, add the double cream and bring the sauce back to the boil, reduce slightly to thicken the sauce. Remove the pan from the heat add the chives and 2 ounces of the remaining butter, stirring the sauce continually to incorporate the butter, add salt and pepper to season.

For the scallops:

In a heavy pan heat the olive oil until hot, season the scallops with salt and pepper , and carefully seal in the hot oil. After 30 seconds turn the scallops.

For the spinach:

Heat the last of the butter in a small pan and add the spinach, season with salt, pepper and nutmeg sauté until hot.

To serve:

Place the spinach on the plates and dress the scallops on the top, gently re-heat the butter sauce (without boiling) and drizzle around the scallops, garnish with some snipped chives and serve.

Acknowledgements

To Chris, Anna and Alexander my family who I adore.

To Mum, where would daughter's be without them.

To Maggie my sister whom Alexander adores.

To Ed Fletcher, owner of Granite City Fish, who has generously financed this book. As his own life has been touched by having a child who has required specialist heart surgery, he has been willing and enthusiastic in supporting another charity.

To Berry and Stuart who do such a fantastic job on the food photography.

To Ottakar's who are supportive, fun and ever willing. Thank you Keith, Gail and especially Alison.

To Mike Reilly, owner of the Olive Tree Restaurant in Aberdeen. I have had a great deal to thank him for, in particular, helping with the organisation of the Book Launch in Aberdeen's Beach Ballroom. I hope he is still talking to me after it!!

To David Barber of Harley & Cox Ltd, the printers of this book. This is my second experience of book printing with David. Hidden Kitchens was very successful, and I hope this will be too.

To Catherine and Jón Ferrier for art work, editing skills and support, I am extremely fortunate to know such gifted people.

To Rose, Brian and Celia at the Autistic Society in Aberdeen, thank you for putting up with me.

To Andrew Stephen from Aberdeen City Council for all his support in the project.

To Sainsbury's Bridge of Dee especially my friend Isabelle Massie, their in house demonstrator for her advice and support.

To Mark Bannerman, Head Chef at the Copthorne Restaurant who so kindly prepared Rick Stein's recipe, for the purposes of photography.

To all the books stores for supporting a second cook book, so soon after Hidden Kitchens of the North.

To Kathy Kyle for all her support.

To Shirley Davis a most loyal and supportive friend.

You know when you feel instantly at ease,
in the company of certain people you meet,
how they instill confidence and put a smile on your face,
and they never make you feel that you're somehow out of place.

Well many years ago, I met a young man,
who lived in a different world from me,
one I did not understand,
but one I was invited in to see.

When I met him, he asked for my name,
and the thing is he'll never forget it,
even if he never sees me again.
At first he would not look me in the eye,
that took a while,
but he's his own man, he's got his own style.

He's into Star Trek and Walkie Talkies and rockets to the moon,
he's got all his favourite things in his bedroom,
he likes to watch news on the TV
in every respect he's a lot like you and me,
during the day, he works to a plan, the only
thing is, its one he doesn't quite understand.

He's certainly a character and he likes to take the mick,
he's often on for a wind up, give and take a bit of stick,
you know that's when the trust comes in,
because he'll look you in the eye,
and let you know a little of what's going on behind.

You know, he puts me instantly at ease,
when I'm in his company I'm never ill at ease,
and when he's sad and wearing a frown,
something's getting him down,
I know I can turn him around and see him smile,
that's why we're friends, and I hope this friendship never ends.

Blair Bell
(Support Worker Partnership)
Aberdeen.

Hotels and Restaurants

Rick Stein
THE SEAFOOD RESTAURANT
Padstow
Cornwall
PL28 8BY
Tel: 01841 532485

ARDOE HOUSE HOTEL
South Deeside Road
Aberdeen
AB12 5YP
Tel: 01224 867355

COCK AND BULL RESTAURANT
Ellon Road
Blairton
Balmedie
Aberdeen
AB23 1XY
Tel: 01358 743249

COPTHORNE HOTEL
122 Huntly Street
Aberdeen
AB10 1SU
Tel: 01224 630404

THE COURTYARD RESTAURANT
1 Alford Lane
Aberdeen
AB1 1YD
Tel: 01224 213795

THE GREEN INN
9 Victoria Road
Ballater
AB35 5QQ
Tel: 01339 755701

THE LAIRHILLOCK
Netherly, By Stonehaven
Aberdeenshire
AB39 3QS
Tel: 01567 730001

THE OLIVE TREE BRASSERIE RESTAURANT
32 Queen's Road
Aberdeen
AB15 6YF
Tel: 01224 208877

SHISH MAHAL RESTAURANT
468 Union Street
Aberdeen
AB10 1TS
Tel: 01224 643339

THE SILVER DARLING RESTAURANT
Porca Quay
North Pier
Aberdeen
AB11 5DQ
Tel: 01224 576229

THAINSTONE HOUSE HOTEL
Inverurie
Aberdeenshire
AB51 5NT
Tel: 01467 621643

THE TOLBOOTH RESTAURANT
Old Pier Road
Stonehaven Harbour
Kincardinshire
AB3 2JU
Tel: 01569 762287

THE UDNY ARMS HOTEL
Main Street
Newburgh
Aberdeenshire
AB41 6BL
Tel: 01358 789444

LOCAL REGIONAL AND NATIONAL AUTISTIC SOCIETIES

Grampian Autistic Society
Royal Cornhill Hospital
Aberdeen AB25 2ZH
General Manager - Brian Walsh
Tel: 01224 840966
Fax: 01224 840967
E-mail: brianwalsh@autism-in-scotland.org.uk

Scottish Society for Autistic Children (SSAC)
SSAC Headquarters
Hilton House
Alloa Business Park
Whins Road
Alloa
FK10 35A
Tel: 01259 720044
Fax: 01259 720051
E-mail: ssac@autism-in-scotland.org.uk

The National Autistic Society
393 City Road
london
EC1V 1NG
United Kingdom
Tel: +44 (0) 171 833 2299
Fax: +44 (0) 171 833 9666
E-mail: nas@nas.org.uk

First Published in 1999 by Mrs Maureen E. Forbes-Gray, Waterton by Ellon,
Aberdeenshire, Scotland, AB41 9QQ
All profits from this publication will be donated to The Grampian Autistic Society

ISBN 0-9533551-1-X

Edited by Maureen Forbes-Gray and Jón Ferrier
Designed by Maureen Forbes-Gray
Cover design Maureen Forbes-Gray and Catherine Coan Ferrier
Front Cover Photographic location, Tolbooth Restaurant, Old Pier, Stonehaven
Printed and Typeset by Harley & Cox Ltd, 4 Shaftesbury Road, Dundee, DD2 1UL

Maureen Forbes-Gray

This is Maureen's fourth cookery book, having an Autistic child herself she understands how complicated the lives are of the families concerned.

With this in mind all the money from this book, after costs, is being donated to the Grampian Autistic Society.

Maureen is a Cordon Bleu trained cook and cookery writer, who is responsible for the publication of this book.

Berry Bingel Photographer www.berrybingel.com

Stuart Johnstone Photographer

Catherine Coan Ferrier Artist and Illustrator

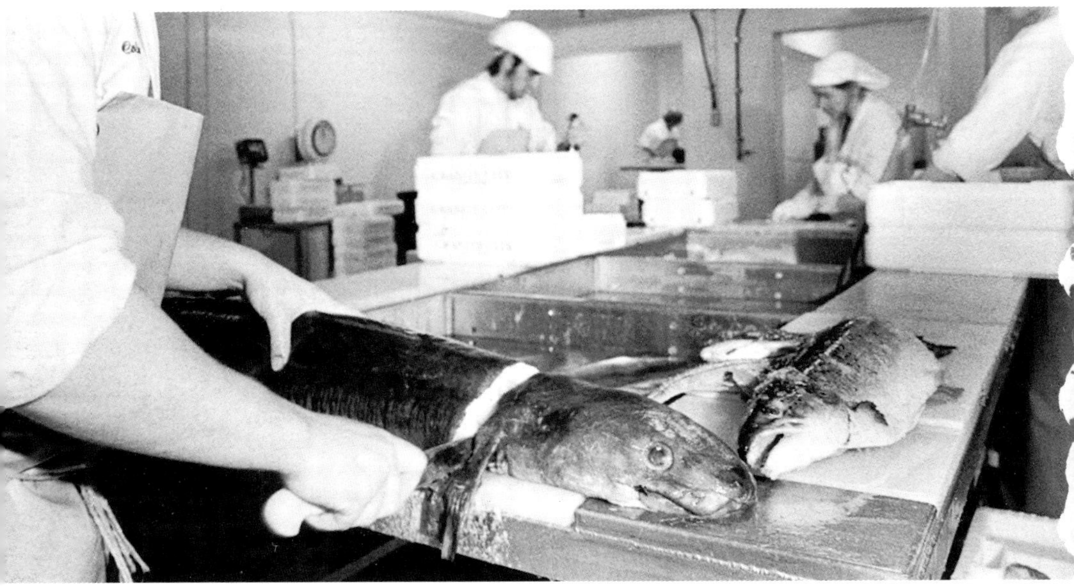